Chi-obaa and Friends

I Talk You Talk Press

CONTENTS

I Talk You Talk Press

INTRODUCTION

MEET CHI-OBAA

These are stories about Chi-obaa, her family and her friends. Chi-obaa has an interesting life. Before you read about Chi-obaa's adventures, I would like you to meet her. You might like to meet her friends and family too.

Mameko Saito lives in Nakashige-cho with her eldest son and his wife. She has three grandchildren.

But no one calls her 'Mameko'. Everyone calls Mameko 'Chi-obaa'. 'Chi-obaa' is short for 'chiisai obaa-san'. 'Chiisai obaa-san' means 'little grandmother' in Japanese.

Her children and grandchildren call her Chi-obaa too. The only person who doesn't call her Chi-obaa, is her daughter-in-law, Kaneko. Kaneko calls her 'okaa-san'. 'Okaa-san' means 'mother' in Japanese.

Chi-obaa is very small. She is 79 years old. Every year she gets smaller, but her energy seems to grow. She is always busy and she is always smiling. Chi-obaa likes bright colours, such as red, pink and purple. Her clothes are very colourful.

Chi-obaa's life was very hard. She was an only child, but when she was 12 years old, her family sent her away from Nakashige-cho. She was sent to Osaka to work in a boarding house. She had to cook and clean for the guests all day. She sent all the money she earned back to her family in Nakashige-cho. When she was 28 years old, she married a man who lived in the boarding house. They had two children. When Chi-obaa was 32 years old, her husband died. Her children were very young. Chi-obaa had no money, so she went back to Nakashige-cho with her children. She cared for her parents, grew vegetables and looked after her children. She worked 16 hours every day. After a few years, her parents died. When Chi-obaa's son was in high school, Chi-obaa sold the land around her house. She wanted money so that her son could go to university. Then she worked as a cleaner for many years.

When Chi-obaa was 65 years old, her son married. He got a good job in the government offices in the city near Nakashige-cho. After he married, he and his wife moved back to his mother's house. When they moved back, Chi-obaa said, "At last! Now I can retire! I've been working for other people all my life. Now I will do everything I want to do for myself."

Chi-obaa has three very important possessions. Her mobile phone, the ipod-nano her grandson gave her when he got an itouch, and her shopping walker. A shopping walker is a bag or box on wheels. Chi-obaa's shopping walker is special. She can carry many things in her walker. It has four wheels, a seat and a brake. Chi-obaa can take a rest anytime by sitting on the walker.

Would you like to meet Chi-obaa's friends and family?

Chi-obaa has two very good friends, Hatsuko and Hanae. They have known each other since they were in primary school.

Hatsuko Nakamura is 79 years old. She married the owner of the barber's shop in Nakashige-cho when she was 22 years old. Hatsuko spent all her life working in the barber's shop. They had three children. One child died when he was very young. When Hatsuko's husband died, her son, Taihei, changed the barber's shop into a fashionable hair salon.

Hatsuko is very tall and thin, and she always wears a hat. She is famous in Nakashige-cho because she is the neighbourhood tama-ire champion. Tama-ire is a competition where teams throw small beanbags into a basket. The basket is on a pole about four metres above the ground. The team with the most goals wins the competition. The towns around Nakashige-cho have a community sports day once a year. All the residents take part in different sporting events. Thanks to Hatsuko, Nakashige-cho always wins the tama-ire competition.

Hanae Yamamoto says she is 70 years old. Chi-obaa and Hatsuko know she is really 78 but they don't say anything. Hanae grew up in

Nakashige-cho, but she moved to Tokyo when she was young. Her mother died and her father left Nakashige-cho and moved to Kyushu, in southern Japan. No one heard anything about Hanae for many years. Then suddenly after more than forty years, Hanae came back to Nakashige-cho. She bought an expensive place in a new apartment block. She seems to have a lot of money. Her clothes are very expensive and she goes to the hairdresser every week, so her hair is always black. She never talks about her years in Tokyo. Chi-obaa and Hatsuko know Hanae has a secret, but they do not ask her questions.

Kenshin Saito is Chi-obaa's eldest son. He works in the local government office. He is a quiet man. People in Nakashige-cho often call him 'Chi-obaa-no-musuko'. This means 'Chi-obaa's son'. Kaneko doesn't like this.

Kaneko is Kenshin's wife. Kaneko and Kenshin met at university in Okayama City. Okayama is Kaneko's hometown. She is a very nice woman and is a good wife and mother. However, her life is difficult because Chi-obaa lives with them. Kaneko cannot understand her mother-in-law. She would like a normal mother-in-law. She complains about Chi-obaa often. She complains to her friends and to her husband. When Kaneko has coffee with her friends, she tells them, "Okaa-san doesn't help with any of the housework. She doesn't cook, clean or do anything to help me! And her clothes are crazy. She is always wearing bright pink clothes! I feel so embarrassed when I see her. And she is always going out. I never know where she is or what she is doing."

Kenshin and Kaneko have three children. Kazuo is studying business at university in Osaka. Yuka is studying fashion in Kobe, and Mitsuru has just started university in Kyushu. Mitsuru wants to be a teacher.

Kazuo, Yuka and Mitsuru like Chi-obaa very much. When they were young, their mother was always busy doing housework and gardening. Chi-obaa didn't help Kaneko at all. She was always free, so she could play with the children every day. Chi-obaa is interested in everything. She is very modern. Kazuo says his grandmother is more like a friend than an old grandmother.

Chi-obaa fills her time with many hobbies. She takes ukulele classes. She goes to a tai-chi group three days a week. She loves movies, surfing the Internet and listening to music. But especially Chi-obaa likes people. She is always out walking and talking to people in Nakashige-cho. People often tell Chi-obaa their secrets. And sometimes Chi-obaa helps people. She believes that sometimes people need a little push to do the right thing. Chi-obaa is good at pushing.

Now you know a little about Chi-obaa, her friends and family, it's time to read some stories about her.

CHI-OBAA AND THE FLOWERS

1. A MYSTERY AND A PLAN

Chi-obaa was pushing her shopping walker down the road. Chi-obaa loves her shopping walker. It is big and it has a brake and a seat. Chi-obaa takes it everywhere. She never goes shopping, but she needs to carry other things.

Today, there was a ukulele in her walker because she was on her way to her ukulele class. She saw her friend Hatsuko looking at a stone wall.

"Good morning, Hatsuko. What are you looking at?"

"I am looking at nothing," answered Hatsuko

"Nothing?" Chi-obaa thought that Hatsuko was having a bad day.

"Yes, nothing!" said Hatsuko. "I should be looking at something, but there's nothing there."

This will take a long time, thought Chi-obaa.

She put the brake on her shopping walker and sat down on the seat. She looked at the wall. There was small shrine in the wall, which contained a statue of Jizo bosatsu. Jizo bosatsu is a Buddhist deity and is known as the protector of children. Especially, of those who died at a young age. The stone statue was wearing a red hat, and in front of it, there was a vase and some small stones.

"What is the nothing I am looking at?" asked Chi-obaa.

"There are no flowers! Every evening I walk here and I put some flowers in front of Jizo bosatsu. Then I pray," said Hatsuko. "Every morning there is one more small stone and no flowers!"

"Why?" asked Chi-obaa.

"Because someone is taking the flowers!"

"When did the flowers start disappearing?" asked Chi-obaa.

"About three weeks ago," answered Hatsuko. "Someone is taking the flowers."

Chi-obaa stood up.

"I must go. I'll be late for my ukulele class. I'll think of a plan. I'll come to your house after my class to discuss what we are going to do about this."

After ukulele class, Chi-obaa went to see Hatsuko in her apartment above the hair salon. Hatsuko made tea and the two old ladies sat down in the living room to talk.

"When do you put the flowers in front of Jizo bosatsu?" asked Chi-obaa.

"Every day about 6:00 or 6:30pm," answered Hatsuko. "And every morning by 9:00am, they are gone."

"Then it's easy, isn't it?" said Chi-obaa. "We just watch the statue between 6:30pm and 9:00am. We will see who takes the flowers and leaves the stone."

"How can we do that?" asked Hatsuko

"I can do it," answered Chi-obaa.

Chi-obaa and Hatsuko made a plan. When Chi-obaa got home, she said to Kaneko, her daughter-in-law, "Nakamura Hatsuko san is not feeling well. I'm going to spend the night with her. I won't eat here tonight."

"I'm sorry to hear that Nakamura san is sick," said Kaneko. "Can I do something to help her? I'm going to the supermarket now. Can I do some shopping for her?"

"No, I think it's OK," said Chi-obaa.

Chi-obaa went to her room. She lay down to rest for a while. When she heard Kaneko go out, she got up. She put a bottle of tea, a blanket, a flashlight, her winter coat and hat into her shopping walker. She charged her mobile phone and her ipod. She cooked some rice and made rice cakes to take as a snack. She put everything into her shopping walker. Then she lay down again. She needed to rest. It was going to be a long night.

At 5:45pm, she heard Kaneko come back from the supermarket. She got up and went downstairs.

"I'm going now," said Chi-obaa. "I'll come back tomorrow morning."

"I hope Nakamura san will soon be well. Please give her my best wishes," said Kaneko.

"I will," said Chi-obaa.

Kaneko went into the kitchen. The rice cooker was still warm and there was the smell of rice in the air.

Why has okaa-san cooked rice? she wondered. That's strange. *Has okaa-san taken rice to her friend's house?* She shook her head and started to unpack the shopping. It was difficult to understand Chi-obaa.

Chi-obaa went to the little shrine with the statue of Jizo bosatsu. Across the road was a children's playground. It had a tall wall made from concrete blocks. Chi-obaa waited until there was no one in the road. Then she pushed her shopping walker behind the wall. She sat down. Some of the concrete blocks had holes in them. She could see the little shrine very well. Chi-obaa waited. At 6:30, Hatsuko came and put flowers in the vase in front of Jizo bosatsu. Then she came into the playground.

"Chi-obaa! Are you OK?" she asked.

"Yes. Yes, of course. Go away! Someone might see you! Don't forget, my daughter- in-law thinks I am staying with you. I told her you are sick."

"I'm going," said Hatsuko. She went out of the playground and down the road to her apartment.

Chi-obaa waited. She watched the shrine through the hole in the wall. She listened to music on her ipod. Chi-obaa likes all kinds of music. Tonight she was listening to American rock music. She thought it might help her to stay awake. Some high school students rode past on their bicycles. They did not stop at the shrine. Some businessmen walked past the shrine on their way home from work. They did not stop either.

Gradually, the light started to fade, and before long, it became dark. The night was cold. Chi-obaa put her coat and hat on. Chi-obaa loves her coat. It is bright pink and very warm. It was her granddaughter Yuka's coat when she was ten years old. When the coat was too small for Yuka, Chi-Obaa took it. Her hat is pink and purple. It had also belonged to Yuka.

At about 10:00pm she ate a rice cake and drank some tea. No one came. Chi-obaa put her blanket around her shoulders. At around 11:00pm, a drunken salaryman on his way home from the local bar staggered past the wall. He did not stop at the shrine. It was getting colder, but Chi-obaa was warm in her coat and hat and blanket. She fell asleep.

2. CHI-OBAA TAKES AN EARLY MORNING WALK

Early next morning, Keita Sato rode along the road past the children's playground. Everyone calls him Keita kun. Keita kun is famous in Nakashige-cho. He is 200cm tall and he is a great basketball player. He has a special bicycle that came from Tokyo. It is a super-size bicycle because he is very tall. Keita kun was going to basketball practice at his school. He is so tall and his bicycle is so big that he could see over the wall. He saw Chi-obaa in a coat and blanket. She was sitting on the seat of her walker. Her head was down.

"Chi-obaa! Chi-obaa! Are you OK?" Keita kun was very worried.

Chi-obaa woke up. She shook her head. "What…? Where am I?"

Then she remembered. "Keita kun! Go away! You didn't see me!"

"But?" Keita kun didn't understand. What was Chi-obaa doing?

"Go!" shouted Chi-obaa.

Keita kun went away.

Chi-obaa looked through the hole in the wall. There were no flowers! Someone had taken the flowers while she was sleeping.

Chi-obaa stood up. She packed everything into her shopping walker. Then she went to Hatsuko's apartment.

"You must be so tired," said Hatsuko.

"No. I'm not so tired. I slept from 11:30pm to 7:30am. But I'm very hungry."

Hatsuko made breakfast.

Hatsuko said, "I'm sorry. You sat in the children's playground all night. But we don't know who takes the flowers. "

"No," said Chi-obaa. "But we do know something."

"What do we know?" asked Hatsuko.

"I think someone takes the flowers in the early morning. I watched until about 11:30pm, but no one took the flowers then. I'll go tomorrow morning very early and I'll watch again."

Chi-obaa went home. "How is Nakamura san?" asked Kaneko.

"Today she is fine," answered Chi-obaa. "But I am worried about my health. I don't want to get sick. I saw on TV that walking is good for older people. Also the man on the TV said that early morning is the best time. Tomorrow I will go out walking very early."

At 5:00am the next morning, Chi-obaa went out of her house. Today she was wearing a red and white tracksuit. It was Yuka's tracksuit when she played volleyball in Junior High School. It is a little too big for Chi-obaa. Chi-obaa was wearing pink and white sneakers and a purple baseball cap. She took her walker. She walked very fast to the children's playground. She went in and sat behind the fence on her walker seat. It was still dark but the sun was rising. Chi-obaa did not have to wait long. At 5:30am, a very small boy walked down the road. He was wearing a jacket, rain boots and pajamas. He was carrying a box. The box was very big for a small boy. He put the box in front of the shrine. He took a small stone out of his pocket. He climbed onto the box and took the flowers. He put the small stone in front of Jizo bosatsu. Then, he climbed down, picked up the box and walked up the road. Very quietly and carefully Chi-obaa followed him.

There was a small cemetery about 100m along the road. The boy left the box at the gate. He walked into the cemetery and stopped at a new tombstone. Chi-obaa followed him. She stood behind a tree. The small boy took the old flowers from the vase on the tombstone and replaced them with the new flowers that he had taken from the shrine. Next he put his hands together and prayed. He took a small stone from the grave and put it in his pocket.

Then he walked back to the road. Chi-obaa walked after him. He picked up his box and walked up a small side street. He went in through a gate and walked down the side of a house. He put the box on the ground next to the wall of the house. He climbed onto the box and then climbed through a window. No one in the house was awake. Chi-obaa stood next to the gate. The name on the gate was Kobayashi. Chi-obaa went back to the cemetery. She looked at the tombstone. It said "Atsuko Kobayashi, aged 35 years". Atsuko Kobayashi had died only 11 months ago.

Chi-obaa went back to the playground. She took her shopping walker and went to Hatsuko's apartment.

She rang the doorbell. The doorbell woke Hatsuko. She opened the door and saw Chi-obaa standing there.

"Do you want breakfast?" she asked.

"Yes, yes, of course," answered Chi-obaa. "And I want you to tell me everything you know about the Kobayashi family. The family that lives up the hill near the cemetery."

Hatsuko made breakfast. She told Chi-obaa about the Kobayashi family. Hatsuko knows a lot about people in Nakashige-cho. She worked for many years in the hairdressers downstairs. In the beginning it was a barbershop. When her husband Shingen died, her son changed the barbershop into a hair salon. Hatsuko still helps in the salon sometimes. Hair salons are good places for news.

"Well," she began. "The owner of the house is Kobayashi Masaki. He married about twelve years ago. A very beautiful girl from Hiroshima …"

3. AN UNHAPPY SALARY MAN AND HIS FAMILY

Masaki Kobayashi was on the train. He was on his way home from work. He worked for an insurance company in the nearby city. Often, since his second marriage, he has felt unhappy on his way home. Will both his wife and son be happy today?

These days his wife is happy. The doctor told her she is pregnant. But his son, Akira, is still very sad. He is a very quiet six-year-old boy. His mother died after a long illness when he was five. When Masaki's first wife was sick in the hospital, he could not look after his son. So Akira went to stay with his grandmother.

His grandmother took Akira to see his mother every day. Masaki went to see his wife every evening. While he was visiting his sick wife, he met a very nice nurse at the hospital. Her name was Reina. They became good friends. Even before his wife died, they talked about marriage. Reina likes children very much. Masaki san thought she would be a good mother for his son, and everyone around him agreed.

"It's a good idea," they said. "You will give your son a mother. You will have someone to look after you."

Now Masaki says, "It was a very bad idea!" But he only says this to himself.

Masaki married Reina four months after his first wife died. He liked her very much. She wanted to be a good mother to his little son. They took the little boy from his grandmother's house. Masaki was very sad about his first wife's death but he was sure he had done the best thing.

But it was terrible. Reina cried, "Your son doesn't like me! I try very hard but he doesn't like me to touch him. He doesn't speak, he doesn't smile."

His son was so quiet. Akira didn't speak to his father, and he never smiled at anyone. Every day he went to school, but he just sat in a corner. He didn't try to join in with the other children or make friends. Masaki had many telephone calls from the school. The schoolteachers were very worried.

Every day, Masaki hoped that life would be better. He hoped that Reina and Akira could be happy. Every day he was disappointed. Then three weeks ago, Reina discovered she was pregnant. Now, she was very happy.

The train stopped at the station and Masaki got off. As Masaki walked from the railway station towards Nakashige-cho, a small hand touched his jacket sleeve. He looked down to see a tiny old woman.

"I want to talk to you," said Chi-obaa.

That evening, Hatsuko took flowers to Jizo bosatsu as usual.

The next morning, as usual, Akira took the flowers, put a small stone in the shrine and went to the cemetery. When he got to the cemetery a very small woman dressed in pink was waiting there.

"Good morning, Akira. Please pray as you always do," she said. "Then we are going to have a picnic breakfast and a nice talk."

"I must go home," said Akira.

"It's OK," said the strange old lady. "Your father knows I am here."

Chi-obaa listened to the unhappy little boy. Akira liked his stepmother but he wanted his mother. He knew his mother had gone but he wanted to remember her. He wanted to hear stories about his mother. His father was always sad if Akira said something about his mother. His stepmother always cried if he asked for his mother.

A little time ago, something had changed in his house. His stepmother, Reina became very happy. She didn't try to talk to Akira, and he became very lonely. He was coming to the graveyard to talk to his mother.

"I understand," Chi-obaa said to Akira. "We will go to your house now. Don't worry."

Chi-obaa took Akira's hand and they walked to his house.

"Is my father angry with me?" asked Akira.

"No. No. He loves you very much. He wants you to be happy."

A few days later, Masaki took Akira to his grandmother's house. He is staying there now and he is happy. He and his grandmother talk about his mother. Every weekend, Masaki goes to spend Sunday with Akira. He tells Akira that he will have a new brother or sister soon. Akira doesn't say anything but he seems to be pleased.

Hatsuko and Chi-obaa know that this result is not perfect. But they are old. They know that perfect is sometimes impossible. Now Hatsuko carries two bunches of flowers every evening. She leaves flowers for her son who died young in front of Jizo bosatsu. And she leaves flowers on the tombstone of Atsuko Kobayashi. She always takes a small stone from the tomb and puts it in front of Jizo bosatsu.

Hatsuko and Chi-obaa know that prayers are answered. They also know it's important to have gratitude.

CHI-OBAA AND THE MAIKO'S SON

1. BREAKFAST AT HANAE'S APARTMENT

(A *maiko* is a trainee geisha.)

Hatsuko Nakamura was cutting Chi-obaa's hair. Hatsuko has retired, although she still helps out in her son's hair salon when it's busy. She always cuts Chi-obaa's hair because they are friends. Chi-obaa's hair is white. Sometimes she likes to put a bow in her hair. The bow is always pink because that's Chi-obaa's favourite colour.

"How's that?" asked Hatsuko.

Chi-obaa looked at herself in the mirror. "It's okay, but it needs a bit of colour. White is so boring. Here, put my pink bow on the top."

Hatsuko put the pink bow in Chi-obaa's snow-white hair.

"That's it!" said Chi-obaa. "Now I look like my normal self!"

Hatsuko laughed. "You are the only 79 year old I know, who wears a pink bow in her hair! Can you imagine Hanae with a bow?"

Hatsuko always cuts and colours Hanae Yamamoto's hair. Hanae has her hair dyed black, and she is always very well-dressed.

"I wonder why Hanae didn't come to Tai Chi today," said Chi-obaa.

"I hope she's OK," answered Hatsuko, looking at Chi-obaa in the mirror. "It's not like her. She never misses Tai Chi practice."

"No," said Chi-obaa. "Perhaps she will come tomorrow."

"I hope so. It's her turn to make breakfast!" said Hatsuko.

Hatsuko, Hanae and Chi-obaa go to Tai Chi at the community centre on Tuesdays, Wednesdays and Thursdays. The Tai Chi group meets at 7:00am. After practice is finished, the three ladies have breakfast together. Sometimes they go to Hatsuko's apartment above the hair salon where Hatsuko prepares a traditional Japanese breakfast. Other times they go to Hanae's beautiful apartment on the third floor of a modern building, next to the river. Hanae serves French bread and pastries with coffee.

They never go to Chi-obaa's house. Chi-obaa lives with her son Kenshin and her daughter-in-law, Kaneko. Kaneko doesn't like having people visit for breakfast. And Chi-obaa doesn't cook any more. When she was 65 years old, she said, "I will retire. I have cooked and cleaned all my life. Now it is time for someone else to do it."

The next day Hanae came to Tai Chi. She said, "Sorry I didn't see you yesterday. Today is my day for breakfast. Please come."

After Tai Chi, the three ladies walked to Hanae's apartment. It was a warm morning, so they sat on the balcony overlooking the river. Hanae san made coffee and they ate delicious pastries from the French bakery. Chi-obaa is always hungry. She enjoyed the pastries very much. But while she was eating, she noticed something odd.

There's something wrong. Hanae is very quiet. She's normally very chatty, she thought.

After breakfast, Hanae said to Chi-obaa and Hatsuko, "Are you busy today? Can you stay a little longer? I want to talk to you both about something."

"It's fine for me," said Hatsuko. "I have no plans."

Chi-obaa took out her diary. It was pink, with pictures of the manga Sailor Moon on it. It was a diary for 2001 that her granddaughter Yuka threw away. Chi-obaa never throws anything away. Chi-obaa hates to waste things. She just writes the correct days and dates in herself. "I have an Italian cooking class at 10:00," she said. "But I can cancel. My cooking partners won't mind."

Hanae and Hatsuko were puzzled. "But you don't cook!" they said.

Chi-obaa smiled. "My cooking partners do all the work," she said. "I like eating the results!"

Chi-obaa called one of her cooking partners on her mobile phone and explained she would not come.

"Now, Hanae. What do you want to talk about?" asked Chi-obaa.

"Come into the living room," answered Hanae.

Hatsuko and Chi-obaa followed Hanae into the living room and sat down. Hanae went to a cabinet and took out a box. She sat on the sofa next to Hatsuko and opened the box.

"Do you remember this?" she asked. She showed Chi-obaa and Hatsuko a photograph.

"Of course I remember!" said Hatsuko. "That's us, on the last day of school."

"Yes," replied Hanae. "It was the last day we were all together."

"We're often together now," said Hatsuko.

"Yes," said Hanae. "But at the end of the summer, that year, I went away and I didn't see you for forty-five years. I didn't write and I didn't come back to Nakashige-cho. But I didn't forget you. Please forgive me. I am sorry."

"I don't know why you are sorry," said Chi-obaa. "I was away from here for twenty years."

"I know," said Hanae. "But you wrote to your parents and came back to visit."

"Only five times in twenty years," said Chi-obaa sadly. "That was all I could do."

"Don't be sorry," said Hatsuko. "But maybe now is a good time to tell Chi-obaa why you didn't come back for so long."

Chi-obaa was surprised. She looked at Hatsuko. "You know?" she asked.

Hatsuko smiled at Hanae. "I can guess a little bit of your story. But only a little."

"I have decided I must tell you my story because I need your help," said Hanae.

2. HANAE'S STORY

"Do you remember when I left Nakashige-cho? I told everyone that I was going to live with my aunt in Tokyo. That was true. My mother was ill. She knew she was dying. My father had a sister in Tokyo and she agreed I could live with her. I told everyone that my aunt would send me to school. That she would pay for me to study to be a secretary. That was my dream. Maybe I believed it," said Hanae.

"The truth was that my aunt had an okiya, a geisha house, in Mukojima. I think she paid my father some money. My mother's medical bills were very high. And you remember, after the war, how expensive everything was."

"Anyway, it was not so bad. My aunt was very kind to me. She wanted me to be a high-class geisha. I didn't do much cleaning and I didn't have to help the senior members of the okiya. Mostly, I went to classes at the geisha school and sat with my aunt in the evenings. I became a maiko in two years. I was fourteen then."

Hanae bent forward so that Chi-obaa could see the top of her head. There was a round spot with no hair.

"That is my mark of honour," said Hanae. "All maiko lose the hair on the top of their head. Did you know what it was, Hatsuko?"

"Yes," said Hatsuko. "I see it when I do your hair. I knew you had been a maiko."

"You didn't say anything," said Hanae.

"No," answered Hatsuko. "It is your business. It is not for me to say."

"I was a maiko for five years," said Hanae. "I didn't come back to

Nakashige-cho to visit. My mother was dead and my father had moved to Kyushu. The entertainment area in Tokyo was like another world. I remembered you and I kept this photograph, but it seemed that you were very far away. My aunt was in no hurry for me to become a full geisha. She wanted to find me a patron. A rich older man who would look after me. The geisha world had changed so much. I think she worried that I would not make enough money to live. But I had an admirer. He was young. He was the son of a geisha from another geisha house. He was a student and he had no money. He was very nice but my aunt would not agree."

"When I was eighteen she found a good patron for me. He was younger than usual patrons and he was very rich. The problem was, I fell in love with him. He said he loved me too. His name was Daijiro. For two more years I stayed in the geisha house. Then I moved into a house he bought for me. I lived in that house for almost forty years until he died."

"He was like your husband," said Hatsuko quietly.

"Yes," said Hanae. "He was. But I was never like his wife. He already had a wife. I was like his mistress."

"In the beginning, I was very happy. I visited my aunt and my other friends. I spent a lot of time having my hair arranged and getting dressed for his visits. Of course I wasn't a maiko anymore, but Daijiro used to like me to dress like one. Then there was a terrible fire in Mukojima. My aunt, and almost everyone I knew, died in the fire. About the same time, I found out I was pregnant. I was so happy! When I told Daijiro, he said he was happy too, but he seemed quiet and strange.

"The next time he came to visit he said, 'My wife knows about you. She has known for a long time. She cannot have children. She says you must give her your baby. I said it is impossible but she says you must.' 'What will happen if I say no?' I asked. 'If you say no, I cannot see you anymore. You cannot live in this house. Please understand. I want a child too. I want a son to take over my company when I am old. Our child will be loved. The child will have everything. You can stay here. I can come to see you. Please say yes. If you say no, I will not see you again.'"

Hatsuko and Chi-obaa looked at Hanae. "What did you do?" asked Chi-obaa.

"Please understand. I had no money. I could not go back to the geisha world. My aunt and everyone I knew was dead. I would have been alone and homeless. I had nothing to give the baby. It was a boy. I gave the baby to Daijiro and his wife and I never saw him again."

"What happened to your lover, Daijiro?" asked Hatsuko.

"I stayed in the house. He came to see me often. We loved each other very much. We were happy in our own way. I lived in that house for thirty-nine years. We never talked about the child I had given to him. Eventually, Daijiro grew old. Then he became ill. He knew he would die. He told me to come back here, to Nakashige-cho, when he died. After he died, I found that he had given me the little house in Tokyo and also a lot of money. I think he was always sorry about taking our son away from me."

"It's a sad story," said Chi-obaa. "But it was a long time ago. Why are you telling us now?"

"Because I need your help. The child knows! He found me. Of course he is a man now. He is fifty-six years old. He wants to meet me!"

3. A PLAN

Hatsuko and Chi-obaa stared at Hanae.

"The son you were forced to give away wants to meet you?" Hatsuko asked.

"Yes, yes!" cried Hanae. "He must hate me. I gave him away!"

"I think you should meet him. If you explain everything, I think he will understand," said Chi-obaa.

She took out her Sailor Moon diary and a pink pencil. "We need to make a plan."

Hanae, Hatsuko and Chi-obaa agreed that it was not a good idea for the son to come to Nakashige-cho. Hatsuko thought that people would see the son. The son might talk to people. "It's not a good idea, Hanae," she said. "You know how people here gossip."

Chi-obaa thought it was a bad idea too. Chi-obaa doesn't care about people gossiping. But she thought there was something strange about the son asking to meet Hanae after so many years. She thought that it would be better if the son didn't find out too much about Hanae. If everything was OK, then Hanae could invite him another time.

"Do you still own the house in Tokyo?" asked Chi-obaa.

"Yes," answered Hanae. "I was too sad to live in it but I couldn't sell it. That's how my son found me."

"What's his name?" asked Hatsuko.

"I don't know what name they gave him," said Hanae. "In the letter he called himself the son of Daijiro Fujita."

"Okay," said Chi-obaa. "How about you meet him in the house in Tokyo?"

"I haven't been there for twenty years!" cried Hanae. "I have an accountant who deals with the house. He does everything, like taxes. I have never even met him. I just pay the bill he sends me every year."

"I think it would be perfect," said Chi-obaa. "You can say to your son, 'this is where you were born.'"

"The house might have fallen down," said Hanae. "It is quite old now. And no one has been looking after it."

"We'll find out!" said Chi-obaa. Hatsuko and Hanae never used a computer, but Chi-obaa was good at computers. Chi-obaa called her house to make sure that daughter-in-law Kaneko was out. She didn't want Kaneko to know what she was doing.

The three women walked through the narrow streets to Chi-obaa's house. Chi-obaa's computer was in her bedroom. It was her grandson Kazuo's old computer. He had set it up for her and she had an Internet connection.

"What do you want a computer for?" Kaneko had asked when Kazuo gave Chi-obaa the computer. "You don't know how to use one."

"I will learn," Chi-obaa had answered.

"But what will you use it for?" Kaneko had asked again.

"Oh, surfing, email….."

"Who would email you?" Kaneko thought her mother-in-law was crazy.

"Maybe you would be surprised," Chi-obaa had answered.

Chi-obaa's computer was on a low table. She sat on a cushion on the floor. Hanae and Hatsuko sat down behind her. Chi-obaa switched on the computer.

"It was a beautiful little house," said Hanae. "Among trees. Next to a shrine. It was very quiet."

"What was the address?" Chi-obaa asked. The computer screen was set to Google maps.

Hanae gave Chi-obaa the address. She typed in the address and pressed the return key.

The three women stared at the screen. They were amazed. The area was full of apartment buildings and hotels, and there was a large motorway running through the town. Chi-obaa switched the map to satellite view. Twenty years ago, there had been trees around the house. There had been a shrine. It had been a quiet rural neighbourhood. Chi-obaa clicked the mouse and zoomed in on the area. The house was still there. There were trees in the small garden. But the house was surrounded by tall buildings and busy streets.

Hanae said nothing. She just stared at the screen. Then suddenly, she stood up.

"It's not the house I remember. So, I don't mind if I meet him there. I'll call my accountant. He has the keys. We will go next week."

"We…?" asked Hatsuko.

"I can't go alone. You're coming with me. We'll take a plane. Today is Wednesday. We'll go on Monday."

The three women were very busy over the next few days.

Hanae took a train to Okayama and bought new clothes in an expensive department store.

Hatsuko cleaned her apartment. She was going to Tokyo on a plane. She might have an accident. The plane might crash. As Hatsuko always says, 'You never know what might happen'. It would be terrible if she was killed and then people went to her apartment and talked about her bad housekeeping. She had her hair styled because going to Tokyo was special occasion, and she borrowed a suitcase from her daughter-in-law.

Chi-obaa sent an email to her grandson, Kazuo. She asked Kazuo if he could find out about Fujita Daijiro, his son and the company. She told her daughter-in-law she was taking a trip.

"Where are you going?" asked Kaneko.

"To Tokyo."

"Why are you going to Tokyo? How will you get there?" asked Kaneko.

"Oh, it's a ladies' club trip. We're going to take a plane," answered Chi-obaa.

"But the Nakashige ladies' club trip this year is to Hiroshima!" Kaneko was surprised. "And you never go on their trips. You say they are boring!"

"This is a different ladies' club," said Chi-Obaa.

Kaneko gave up. Chi-obaa never told her anything. That night, she told her husband. "Your mother is taking a trip to Tokyo. She won't say why she's going," said Kaneko.

"Don't worry. She'll have a great time in Tokyo. Chi-obaa can take care of herself," said Kenshin. Kaneko shook her head. *Why can't I have a normal mother-in-law?* she thought.

Chi-obaa exchanged many emails with Kazuo before the trip.

4. THE MEETING

On Monday, Hanae, Hatsuko and Chi-obaa went to the airport. Hatsuko's son drove them. It was a big occasion. Hanae takes an overseas trip every year, but Chi-obaa and Hatsuko had not been on an airplane before.

"Are you nervous?" asked Taihei, Hatsuko's son, the hairdresser

Hatsuko didn't answer. She felt sick.

Hanae looked at Hatsuko.

"You'll be fine Hatsuko. It's very easy to take a plane. You'll enjoy it."

Hanae looked at Chi-obaa. Chi-obaa looked worried.

Is Chi-obaa worried about flying? thought Hanae. *I didn't think Chi-obaa was frightened of anything!*

The trip to Tokyo went smoothly. When they arrived, the three women had an early lunch in the airport. Then they took the train to Shinjuku and then another train to Urawa. Hanae found a taxi at Urawa Station.

Hatsuko climbed into the taxi. She sat next to Chi-obaa. The flight was wonderful and Hatsuko forgot to be scared. The train ride from Haneda Airport had been good too. But now Hatsuko was feeling tired. Everything was noisy, busy and dirty. There were too many people. *Of course Chi-obaa loves this kind of place,* she thought.

She looked at Chi-obaa. Chi-obaa looked worried.

I wonder what the problem is, thought Hatsuko. *I thought she would be very excited.*

"My accountant has gone to the house," said Hanae. "My son will

25

be there too. They are expecting us at 2:30pm."

It was 2:20 when the taxi stopped outside the little house. It looked very strange. It was surrounded by tall buildings and the road outside was full of cars. There were trees all around the house. Hanae opened the wooden gate and they walked into the garden. The garden was very tidy. The branches of all the trees had been neatly trimmed, and there were some flowers growing in the flower beds.

"A gardener must come here often," said Hatsuko.

"I don't pay for a gardener," said Hanae. She was very puzzled.

The house was a traditional Japanese style building, with a verandah leading to the garden. The verandah had glass doors and wooden steps. Two men were sitting on the steps.

As the three women walked towards the house one of the men stood up. He was an old man. He was very handsome. "Yamamoto san?" he said, looking at Hanae. "I am Suzuki, your accountant." He bowed.

Hanae introduced Hatsuko and Chi-obaa. Then everyone turned to the man who was sitting on the steps. He was a big man. He was wearing a dark suit. He just looked at them. He did not stand up. He looked at the three old women in front of him. One was dressed in a bright tracksuit with pink running shoes, one was tall and thin, and looked like a typical grandmother, and the other one…he looked at her eyes, and he knew immediately.

He pointed at Hanae. "You are Hanae Yamamoto ?" he asked.

Hanae nodded her head.

You are my mother?"

Hanae nodded again. Her face was very pale and she was shaking. The man was talking to her like a policeman.

Suzuki san looked very unhappy. "Please, Fujita san. The ladies have had a long journey. Let us go inside. I have arranged for some tea."

Suzuki san unlocked the door. They went into the house. The tatami mats were very old, but very clean. There was new shoji paper on the sliding paper screens, and someone had put a spray of flowers in the reception room. There were cushions on the floor. On a small table there was a jug of hot water, a tea pot, tea and some cups.

Hanae, the two men and Chi-obaa knelt down on the cushions, while Hatsuko prepared the tea.

No one spoke. Hatsuko poured the green tea into the cups, and handed one to each person. Hanae took a nervous sip of her tea.

After a few moments, Hanae turned to her son. "I am so pleased to see you," she said to him.

He looked at her. "Why did my father give you this house? It should belong to my family. I want it back."

Everyone was shocked.

"Fujita san. This should be a happy occasion. This is your mother. Please do not speak like this. It is not a good way to speak," said Suzuki san. He frowned at Fujita san.

Tears started to run down Hanae's cheeks. "Your father and I were good friends for many years. He bought this house for me to live in. I lived here for almost forty years. He wanted me to have this house."

"I want this house. My father was weak and stupid. I have brought the papers with me. You can sign them now."

Hanae looked at Chi-obaa. Very carefully, Chi-obaa shook her head. Hanae looked at her son again. He had not wanted to meet her. He was only interested in the house. Hanae felt sad. She could understand that her son might hate her, but it was wrong of him to say bad things about his father. Hanae thought about Daijiro and the love they had shared. This gave Hanae courage.

She looked at her son with anger in her eyes.

"I have cried for you for fifty-six years! Do you think I wanted to give you up? I did it because I loved you. Because I didn't have anything to give you. Every day of my life since you were born I have been sorry. But now I've met you. You have no respect for your father. I am ashamed you are my son!"

"You feel strong because your friends are here. I thought you would come alone. You say you didn't have anything to give me. Well now you do. You can give me this house," her son answered.

Suzuki san stood up. "Fujita san. I made a bad mistake in arranging this meeting. I am ashamed. I thought you wanted to meet your mother. I thought it would be a day of happiness. All you wanted was to take this house from her. This is not your house. This is the house of Hanae Yamamoto. Please leave."

Fujita san stood up. He looked at them all for a few seconds, then, in silence, he walked out of the house.

5. WHAT HANAE DID NEXT

Hatsuko got up and served more tea. Hanae and Suzuki san sat down again. Suzuki san turned to Hanae.

"I am so sorry. I am your accountant. But I am a foolish old man. Fujita san found the legal papers from when his father bought this house and when he changed the ownership to you. It was my company that did the work. Of course, when he bought the house, I was only a student. When I graduated, I joined this company, and now I own it. Please forgive me. I should not have told him how to find you. I am so sorry. He is your son, but I don't think he is a nice man."

Then Chi-obaa spoke. "I have something to tell you. I thought it was very strange that Fujita san found you and wanted to meet. I thought there was something wrong. I hoped I had made a mistake. I hoped this would be a happy day. But I don't trust people. I think there are many bad people in the world. I asked my grandson to check on the Fujita family company. They are in big trouble. They need money soon. That man, your son, Hanae, is a gambler. He has lost a lot of family money. He has no money to save the company."

"I am sorry, Hanae. You must be very unhappy," said Hatsuko. She reached out and touched Hanae's hand.

"I am so sorry too," said Suzuki san. "I wanted to give you happiness. You see, when Fujita Daijiro came to see me to change the ownership of the house before he died, he told me the story."

Hanae didn't say anything. She drank her tea and looked out the window at the flowers in the garden. The others sat and watched her.

28

Then Hanae spoke. "The house is in good condition. The garden is cared for. I never paid for that." She looked at Suzuki san. "Did you do this?"

Suzuki san looked at the floor. He was embarrassed. Hanae reached out and touched his hand.

"I know who you are," she said. "I knew who you were, as soon as I saw you. You are the son of the great geisha, O-michizono. I knew you when we were both very young. You were my first love."

Suzuki san looked at Hanae. "I was only twenty when your aunt found Fujita Daijiro for you. I was in love with you but I couldn't do anything," he said quietly. "I went away to university. I thought you died in the fire with your aunt. You can imagine how I felt when Fujita san came to me to discuss money for you and changing the ownership of the house. It was a miracle. He told me the story. He asked me to be careful about your money and the house," Suzuki san explained.

"So you cared for the house?" asked Hanae.

"Yes. You had been happy here. I wanted to keep it for you."

Hanae smiled and touched his hand again. "You have been a good friend. I am very lucky to have a friend like you."

It had been a very hard day. Everyone was tired. Hanae said goodbye to Suzuki san. She agreed to meet him the next day to discuss business. That night Hanae, Hatsuko and Chi-obaa stayed in a hotel in Shinjuku. They went to bed early.

The next morning at breakfast, Chi-obaa said, "What time will we meet Suzuki san?"

Hanae looked at the window. She didn't look at Chi-obaa.

"Why don't you and Hatsuko go shopping?" she said. "I will go to see Suzuki san alone."

Chi-obaa was surprised. "Are you sure?"

"Yes. You and Hatsuko can have a nice time. Enjoy Tokyo."

Hatsuko was not sure. Tokyo made her tired and nervous. She wondered what shopping with Chi-obaa would be like. Chi-obaa never bought anything.

"I don't want to go shopping," said Chi-obaa. "I want to go to Disneyland. Come with me to Disneyland Hatsuko!"

The hotel had a limousine bus to Disneyland, and they bought tickets at the hotel reception. Hatsuko and Chi-obaa had a wonderful time at Disneyland. When they got back to the hotel it was 6:00pm.

Hanae was not there. They waited impatiently for her in the lobby.

At 10:00pm, Hanae walked through the doors.

Chi-obaa and Hatsuko jumped up and ran to meet her.

"At last! Where have you been?" asked Hatsuko. "We were worried about you! Yesterday was a very bad day for you. Are you OK?"

Hanae smiled. "I had a very nice day today. I have decided to give the house to my son."

"What?" cried Hatsuko. "Are you crazy? I am sorry Hanae, but he is not a nice man. Why would you give him your house?"

"But he is my son," answered Hanae. "And he needs the money. I think Daijiro would want me to do this."

Hatsuko didn't say anything.

"What about Suzuki san?" asked Chi-obaa. "Is he unhappy? He looked after the house for you. And now you are going to give it away."

Hanae san's face was a little pink. "I went to the house to say goodbye to Daijiro and my memories. Suzuki san came with me. He brought two bento lunch boxes for us. We sat in the house all day and talked and talked."

"And…?" Chi-obaa wanted more information.

Hanae's face was red now. "He said that spending one day there with me was his reward."

Chi-obaa laughed. "And he plans a trip to Nakashige, sometime soon!"

Hanae looked down at her hands. "He didn't say. But he told me he plans to retire soon. His wife died a few years ago. His son is in America. I think he is lonely."

"How do you feel about your son, now?" asked Hatsuko. She thought that Hanae was crazy but she promised herself she would not say anything about the house.

"I have cried for him every day since Daijiro took him away from me. Now I have seen him. I have seen the man he has become. I won't cry for him anymore."

Chi-obaa looked at Hanae. "You will never give him anything else, will you?"

Hanae looked very sad. "He thinks the house is all I had. He doesn't know about the money. I didn't tell him. He thinks he has taken everything from me. I won't see him again."

"Good!" said Chi-obaa. "Now in my room there is a refrigerator. There is a bottle of sake in the refrigerator. We should have a little party, because it's the first time we have ever taken a trip together!"

They sat on Chi-obaa's bed. "You are paying for the sake, Hanae," said Chi-obaa. "You should make the toast."

Hanae looked at her friends. She looked at Hatsuko, tall, thin and wearing grandmother clothes. She looked at tiny Chi-obaa in her secondhand running shoes and best secondhand track suit. In the mirror on the wall, she could see herself; medium height, a little plump, and very elegant.

"To friends," she said and raised her glass. "Family can be disappointing but friends are always friends."

THANK YOU

Thank you for reading Chi-obaa and Friends. (Word count: 8,866)
We hope you enjoyed it. We have two more graded readers with
stories from Nakashige-cho:
Chi-obaa and Her Town
The Witches of Nakashige

There are quizzes about this book on our free study site I Talk You
Talk Press EXTRA. http://italk-youtalk.com

If you would like to read more graded readers, please visit our
website
http://www.italkyoutalk.com

Other Level 4 graded readers include
Chi-obaa and Her Town
End House (Old Secrets – Modern Mysteries Book 2)
On the Run (Old Secrets – Modern Mysteries Book 3)
The Blue Lace Curtain (Old Secrets – Modern Mysteries Book 1)
The Legacy
The Witches of Nakashige
Vanished Away

ABOUT THE AUTHOR

I Talk You Talk Press is a Japan-based publisher of language textbooks, graded readers and language learning/teaching resources.

Our team is made up of highly experienced language teachers and translators, who have all studied at least one additional language to an advanced level.

This experience enables us to design our materials from the perspective of both the teacher and the learner. We consult with both teachers and language learners when designing our textbooks and graded readers, and test our materials extensively in the classroom before publication.

We are a fast-growing press, and currently publish graded readers for learners of English. We publish new graded readers monthly.